FOR:_____

*I*f any of you lacks wisdom, he should ask God,
who gives generously to all.

James 1:5

FROM:

WORDS OF
WISDOM FOR
A WOMAN
OF FAITH

Zondervan*Gifts*

We have a gift for inspiration™

WORDS OF WISDOM FOR A WOMAN OF FAITH ON

THE VALUE OF WISDOM

*I*f any of you lacks wisdom, he should ask God, who gives generously to all without finding fault, and it will be given to him.

James 1:5

❧

*B*ut the wisdom that comes from heaven is first of all pure; then peace-loving, considerate, submissive, full of mercy and good fruit, impartial and sincere.

James 3:17

*T*he fear of the LORD is the beginning of wisdom,
and knowledge of the Holy One is understanding.

Proverbs 9:10

❧

*H*e will be the sure foundation for your times, a
rich store of salvation and wisdom and knowledge;
the fear of the LORD is the key to this treasure.

Isaiah 33:6

Get wisdom, get understanding; do not forget my words or swerve from them. Do not forsake wisdom, and she will protect you; love her, and she will watch over you. Wisdom is supreme; therefore get wisdom. Though it cost all you have, get understanding. Esteem her, and she will exalt you; embrace her, and she will honor you. She will set a garland of grace on your head and present you with a crown of splendor.

Proverbs 4:5–9

$\mathcal{C}$hoose my instruction instead of silver, knowledge rather than choice gold, for wisdom is more precious than rubies, and nothing you desire can compare with her. "I, wisdom, dwell together with prudence; I possess knowledge and discretion."

Proverbs 8:10–12

❧

$\mathcal{F}$or I will give you words and wisdom that none of your adversaries will be able to resist or contradict.

Luke 21:15

*H*ow much better to get wisdom than gold,
to choose understanding rather than silver!

Proverbs 16:16

*B*uy the truth and do not sell it; get wisdom,
discipline and understanding.

Proverbs 23:23

*W*isdom, like an inheritance, is a good thing
and benefits those who see the sun. Wisdom
is a shelter as money is a shelter, but the
advantage of knowledge is this: that wisdom
preserves the life of its possessor.

Ecclesiastes 7:11–12

$\mathcal{H}$appy are those who find wisdom, and those who get understanding, for her income is better than silver, and her revenue better than gold. She is more precious than jewels, and nothing you desire can compare with her. Long life is in her right hand; in her left hand are riches and honor. Her ways are ways of pleasantness, and all her paths are peace. She is a tree of life to those who lay hold of her; those who hold her fast are called happy.

Proverbs 3:13–18 (NRSV)

*M*y purpose is that they may be encouraged in heart and united in love, so that they may have the full riches of complete understanding, in order that they may know the mystery of God, namely, Christ, in whom are hidden all the treasures of wisdom and knowledge.

Colossians 2:2–3

INTEGRITY

$\mathcal{L}$ORD, who may dwell in your sanctuary? Who may live on your holy hill? He whose walk is blameless and who does what is righteous, who speaks the truth from his heart and has no slander on his tongue, who does his neighbor no wrong and casts no slur on his fellowman.

Psalm 15:1–3

$\mathcal{T}$he man of integrity walks securely,
but he who takes crooked paths
will be found out.

Proverbs 10:9

❧

$\mathcal{T}$he integrity of the upright guides them, but the
unfaithful are destroyed by their duplicity.

Proverbs 11:3

*M*ay integrity and uprightness protect me,
because my hope is in you.

Psalm 25:21

❧

*B*etter to be poor and walk in integrity than to
be crooked in one's ways even though rich.

Proverbs 28:6 (NRSV)

$\mathcal{L}$et love and faithfulness never leave you; bind them around your neck, write them on the tablet of your heart. Then you will win favor and a good name in the sight of God and man.

Proverbs 3:3–4

$\mathcal{A}$ good name is more desirable than great riches; to be esteemed is better than silver or gold.

Proverbs 22:1

❧

$\mathcal{A}$ good name is better than fine perfume.

Ecclesiates 7:1

SPEECH

*H*e who guards his lips guards his life,
but he who speaks rashly will come to ruin.
Proverbs 13:3

❧

A gentle answer turns away wrath, but
a harsh word stirs up anger.
Proverbs 15:1

*T*he tongue of the righteous is choice silver,
but the heart of the wicked is of little value.
The lips of the righteous nourish many, but
fools die for lack of judgment.

Proverbs 10:20–21

$\mathscr{D}$o not be quick with your mouth, do not be hasty in your heart to utter anything before God. God is in heaven and you are on earth, so let your words be few. When you make a vow to God, do not delay in fulfilling it. He has no pleasure in fools; fulfill your vow. It is better not to vow than to make a vow and not fulfill it.

Ecclesiastes 5:2,4–5

*W*hoever of you loves life and desires to see many good days, keep your tongue from evil and your lips from speaking lies.

Psalm 34:12–13

❧

A gossip goes about telling secrets, but one who is trustworthy in spirit keeps a confidence.

Proverbs 11:13 (NRSV)

*M*y dear brothers, take note of this: Everyone should be quick to listen, slow to speak and slow to become angry, for man's anger does not bring about the righteous life that God desires.

James 1:19–20

*I*f anyone considers himself religious and yet does not keep a tight rein on his tongue, he deceives himself and his religion is worthless.

James 1:26

$\mathcal{K}$eep reminding them of these things. Warn them before God against quarreling about words; it is of no value, and only ruins those who listen. Avoid godless chatter, because those who indulge in it will become more and more ungodly.

2 Timothy 2:14, 16

*I*n your hearts set apart Christ as Lord. Always be prepared to give an answer to everyone who asks you to give the reason for the hope that you have. But do this with gentleness and respect, keeping a clear conscience, so that those who speak maliciously against your good behavior in Christ may be ashamed of their slander.

1 Peter 3:15–16

*S*peak to one another with psalms, hymns
and spiritual songs. Sing and make music in
your heart to the Lord, always giving thanks to
God the Father for everything, in the name
of our Lord Jesus Christ.

Ephesians 5:19–20

*L*et your conversation be always full of
grace, seasoned with salt, so that you may
know how to answer everyone.

Colossians 4:6

*W*ith the tongue we praise our Lord and Father, and with it we curse men, who have been made in God's likeness. Out of the same mouth come praise and cursing. My brothers, this should not be. Can both fresh water and salt water flow from the same spring?

James 3:9–11

❧

*S*et a guard over my mouth, O LORD; keep watch over the door of my lips.

Psalm 141:3

❧

*M*y tongue will speak of your righteousness and of your praises all day long.

Psalm 35:28

CONDUCT

$\mathscr{D}$ear friends, I urge you . . . to abstain from sinful desires, which war against your soul. Live such good lives among the pagans that, though they accuse you of doing wrong, they may see your good deeds and glorify God.

1 Peter 2:11–12

*E*ven a child is known by his actions, by whether
his conduct is pure and right.

Proverbs 20:11

*D*on't let anyone look down on you
because you are young, but set an example
for the believers in speech, in life, in love,
in faith and in purity.

1 Timothy 4:12

$\mathcal{S}$ince we live by the Spirit, let us keep in step
with the Spirit. Let us not become conceited,
provoking and envying each other.

Galatians 5:25–26

❧

$\mathcal{B}$e wise in the way you act toward outsiders;
make the most of every opportunity.

Colossians 4:5

$\mathcal{F}$or the grace of God that brings salvation
has appeared to all men. It teaches us to say "No"
to ungodliness and worldly passions,
and to live self-controlled, upright and godly
lives in this present age.

Titus 2:11–12

$\mathcal{I}$ have been crucified with Christ and I no
longer live, but Christ lives in me. The life I live
in the body, I live by faith in the Son of God,
who loved me and gave himself for me.

Galatians 2:20

*O*ur conscience testifies that we have conducted
ourselves in the world . . . in the holiness
and sincerity that are from God. We have done
so not according to worldly wisdom but
according to God's grace.

2 Corinthians 1:12

*R*emember your leaders, who spoke the word
of God to you. Consider the outcome of their
way of life and imitate their faith.

Hebrews 13:7

*B*lessed is the man who does not walk in the counsel of the wicked or stand in the way of sinners or sit in the seat of mockers. But his delight is in the law of the Lord, and on his law he meditates day and night. He is like a tree planted by streams of water, which yields its fruit in season and whose leaf does not wither. Whatever he does prospers.

Psalm 1:1–3

*F*inally, brothers, whatever is true, whatever is noble, whatever is right, whatever is pure, whatever is lovely, whatever is admirable—if anything is excellent or praiseworthy— think about such things. Whatever you have learned or received or heard from me, or seen in me—put it into practice. And the God of peace will be with you.

Philippians 4:8–9

POLITICS/
GOVERNMENT

*B*lessed is the nation whose God is the LORD.
Psalm 33:12

*I*f my people, who are called by my name,
will humble themselves and pray and seek my
face and turn from their wicked ways, then will
I hear from heaven and will forgive their sin
and will heal their land.
2 Chronicles 7:14

*E*veryone must submit himself to the governing
authorities, for there is no authority except that
which God has established. The authorities that
exist have been established by God.
Romans 13:1

$\mathcal{I}$ urge, then, first of all, that requests, prayers, intercession and thanksgiving be made for everyone—for . . . all those in authority, that we may live peaceful and quiet lives in all godliness and holiness. This is good, and pleases God our Savior, who wants all men to be saved and to come to a knowledge of the truth.

1 Timothy 2.1–4

$\mathcal{S}$ubmit yourselves for the Lord's sake to every authority instituted among men. For it is God's will that by doing good you should silence the ignorant talk of foolish men.

1 Peter 2:13,15

❧

$\mathcal{S}$peak up for those who cannot speak for themselves, for the rights of all who are destitute. Speak up and judge fairly; defend the rights of the poor and needy.

Proverbs 31:8–9

GOD'S WILL

*T*each me to do your will, for you are my God;
may your good Spirit lead me on level ground.

Psalm 143:10

❧

*D*o not conform any longer to the pattern
of this world, but be transformed by the renewing
of your mind. Then you will be able to test
and approve what God's will is—his good,
pleasing and perfect will.

Romans 12:2

*I*t is God's will that you should be sanctified:
that you should avoid sexual immorality; that
each of you should learn to control his own body
in a way that is holy and honorable, and that in
this matter no one should wrong his brother or
take advantage of him. For God did not call us to
be impure, but to live a holy life.

1 Thessalonians 4:3–4,7

*T*herefore do not be foolish, but understand what the Lord's will is. Do not get drunk on wine, which leads to debauchery. Instead, be filled with the Spirit. Speak to one another with psalms, hymns and spiritual songs. Sing and make music in your heart to the Lord, always giving thanks to God the Father for everything, in the name of our Lord Jesus Christ. Submit to one another out of reverence for Christ.

Ephesians 5:17–21

$\mathcal{F}$or it is God's will that by doing good you should silence the ignorant talk of foolish people.

1 Peter 2:15

❧

$\mathcal{G}$ive thanks in all circumstances, for this is God's will for you in Christ Jesus.

1 Thessalonians 5:18

*W*e have confidence before God and receive from him anything we ask, because we obey his commands and do what pleases him. And this is his command: to believe in the name of his Son, Jesus Christ, and to love one another as he commanded us.

1 John 3:21–22

*T*he world and its desire are passing away, but those who do the will of God live forever.

1 John 2:17 (NRSV)

PRAYER

$\mathcal{D}$evote yourselves to prayer, being watchful and thankful.

Colossians 4:2

$\mathcal{I}$f I had cherished sin in my heart, the Lord would not have listened; but God has surely listened and heard my voice in prayer.

Psalm 66:18–19

$\mathcal{T}$herefore confess your sins to each other and pray for each other so that you may be healed. The prayer of a righteous man is powerful and effective.

James 5:16

$\mathcal{I}$s any one of you in trouble? He should pray. Is anyone happy? Let him sing songs of praise. Is any one of you sick? He should call the elders of the church to pray over him and anoint him with oil in the name of the Lord. And the prayer offered in faith will make the sick person well; the Lord will raise him up. If he has sinned, he will be forgiven.

James 5:13–15

$\mathcal{S}$o I say to you: Ask and it will be given to you; seek and you will find; knock and the door will be opened to you. For everyone who asks receives; he who seeks finds; and to him who knocks, the door will be opened.

Luke 11:9–10

*J*esus said, "Therefore I tell you, whatever you ask for in prayer, believe that you have received it, and it will be yours. And when you stand praying, if you hold anything against anyone, forgive him, so that your Father in heaven may forgive you your sins."

Mark 11:24–25

*J*esus said, "I will do whatever you ask in my name, so that the Son may bring glory to the Father. You may ask me for anything in my name, and I will do it."

John 14:13–14

❧

*T*his is the confidence we have in approaching God: that if we ask anything according to his will, he hears us. And if we know that he hears us—whatever we ask—we know that we have what we asked of him.

1 John 5:14–15

FAITH &
FAITHFULNESS

*N*ow faith is being sure of what we hope for
and certain of what we do not see.
Hebrews 11:1

*S*o we fix our eyes not on what is seen, but on
what is unseen. For what is seen is temporary, but
what is unseen is eternal.
2 Corinthians 4:18

*W*e live by faith, not by sight.
2 Corinthians 5:7

*T*hough you have not seen him, you love him;
and even though you do not see him now, you
believe in him and are filled with an inexpressible
and glorious joy, for you are receiving the goal of
your faith, the salvation of your souls.

1 Peter 1:8–9

*J*esus answered, "The work of God is this: to believe in the one he has sent."

John 6:29

❦

*T*hen Jesus told him, "Because you have seen me, you have believed; blessed are those who have not seen and yet have believed."

John 20:29

❦

*F*or it is by grace you have been saved, through faith—and this not from yourselves, it is the gift of God.

Ephesians 2:8

$\mathcal{I}$f you confess with your mouth, "Jesus is Lord," and believe in your heart that God raised him from the dead, you will be saved. For it is with your heart that you believe and are justified, and it is with your mouth that you confess and are saved.

Romans 10:9–10

$\mathscr{D}$ear friend, you are faithful in what you
are doing for the brothers, even though
they are strangers to you.

3 John 1:5

$\mathscr{K}$now therefore that the LORD your God is God;
he is the faithful God, keeping his covenant of
love to a thousand generations of those who love
him and keep his commands.

Deuteronomy 7:9

SERVICE

I thank Christ Jesus our Lord, who has given me strength, that he considered me faithful, appointing me to his service.

1 Timothy 1:12

*J*esus said, "Whoever serves me must follow me; and where I am, my servant also will be. My Father will honor the one who serves me."

John 12:26

*S*erve the LORD with fear and
rejoice with trembling.
Psalm 2:11

❧

*W*hatever you do, work at it with all your
heart, as working for the Lord, not for men,
since you know that you will receive an
inheritance from the Lord as a reward. It is
the Lord Christ you are serving.
Colossians 3:23–24

*N*ever be lacking in zeal, but keep your spiritual fervor, serving the Lord. Be joyful in hope, patient in affliction, faithful in prayer. Share with God's people who are in need. Practice hospitality.

Romans 12:11–13

❧

*B*ut now, by dying to what once bound us, we have been released from the law so that we serve in the new way of the Spirit, and not in the old way of the written code.

Romans 7:6

*W*ho is wise and understanding among you? Let him show it by his good life, by deeds done in the humility that comes from wisdom.

James 3:13

*A*nd do not forget to do good and to share with others, for with such sacrifices God is pleased.

Hebrews 13:16

$\mathcal{N}$o one can serve two masters. Either he will hate the one and love the other, or he will be devoted to the one and despise the other. You cannot serve both God and Money.

Matthew 6:24

$\mathcal{R}$eligion that God our Father accepts as pure and faultless is this: to look after orphans and widows in their distress and to keep oneself from being polluted by the world.

James 1:27

SEXUAL
PURITY

$\mathcal{D}$aughters of Jerusalem, I charge you by the gazelles and by the does of the field: Do not arouse or awaken love until it so desires.

Song of Songs 3:5

$\mathcal{H}$ow can a young man keep his way pure? By living according to your word.

Psalm 119:9

$\mathcal{B}$lessed are the pure in heart, for they will see God.

Matthew 5:8

"*E*verything is permissible for me"— but not everything is beneficial. "Everything is permissible for me"— but I will not be mastered by anything. "Food for the stomach and the stomach for food"— but God will destroy them both. The body is not meant for sexual immorality, but for the Lord, and the Lord for the body.

1 Corinthians 6:12–13

*F*lee the evil desires of youth, and pursue righteousness, faith, love and peace, along with those who call on the Lord out of a pure heart.

2 Timothy 2:22

❧

*M*arriage should be honored by all, and the marriage bed kept pure, for God will judge the adulterer and all the sexually immoral.

Hebrews 13:4

Flee from sexual immorality. All other sins a man commits are outside his body, but he who sins sexually sins against his own body. Do you not know that your body is a temple of the Holy Spirit, who is in you, whom you have received from God? You are not your own; you were bought at a price. Therefore honor God with your body.

1 Corinthians 6:18–20

$\mathcal{D}$o not be yoked together with unbelievers. For what do righteousness and wickedness have in common? Or what fellowship can light have with darkness? What harmony is there between Christ and Belial? What does a believer have in common with an unbeliever?

2 Corinthians 6:14–15

❧

LOVE

*F*or as high as the heavens are above the earth,
so great is God's love for those who fear him.

Psalm 103:11

❧

*B*e imitators of God, therefore, as dearly loved
children and live a life of love, just as Christ loved
us and gave himself up for us as a fragrant
offering and sacrifice to God.

Ephesians 5:1–2

To love God with all your heart, with all your understanding and with all your strength, and to love your neighbor as yourself is more important than all burnt offerings and sacrifices.

Mark 12:33

Christs' command is this: "Love each other as I have loved you. Greater love has no one than this, that he lay down his life for his friends."

John 15:12–13

*I*f you have any encouragement from being
united with Christ, if any comfort from his love,
if any fellowship with the Spirit, if any tenderness
and compassion, then make my joy complete by
being like-minded, having the same love, being
one in spirit and purpose. Do nothing out of
selfish ambition or vain conceit, but in humility
consider others better than yourselves. Each of
you should look not only to your own interests,
but also to the interests of others.

Philippians 2:1–4

*I*f I speak in the tongues of men and of angels, but have not love, I am only a resounding gong or a clanging cymbal. If I have the gift of prophecy and can fathom all mysteries and all knowledge, and if I have a faith that can move mountains, but have not love, I am nothing. If I give all I possess to the poor and surrender my body to the flames, but have not love, I gain nothing.

1 Corinthians 13:1–3

$\mathcal{L}$ove is patient, love is kind. It does not envy, it does not boast, it is not proud. It is not rude, it is not self-seeking, it is not easily angered, it keeps no record of wrongs. Love does not delight in evil but rejoices with the truth. It always protects, always trusts, always hopes, always perseveres. Love never fails. And now these three remain: faith, hope and love. But the greatest of these is love.

1 Corinthians 13:4–8, 13

RELATIONSHIPS
AND
RESPONSIBILITIES

MARRIAGE

For this reason a man will leave his father and mother and be united to his wife, and the two will become one flesh. So they are no longer two, but one. Therefore what God has joined together, let man not separate.

Matthew 19:5–6

He who finds a wife finds what is good and receives favor from the LORD.

Proverbs 18:22

A wife of noble character is her
husband's crown.

Proverbs 12:4

*H*ouses and wealth are inherited from parents,
but a prudent wife is from the LORD.

Proverbs 19:14

*W*ives, in the same way be submissive to your
husbands so that, if any of them do not believe
the word, they may be won over without words
by the behavior of their wives, when they see the
purity and reverence of your lives.

1 Peter 3:1–2

CHILDREN

God blessed them and said to them, "Be
fruitful and increase in number; fill the earth
and subdue it. Rule over the fish of the sea
and the birds of the air and over every living
creature that moves on the ground."

Genesis 1:28

❧

Sons are a heritage from the LORD,
children a reward from him.

Psalm 127:3

$\mathcal{A}$ woman giving birth to a child has pain because her time has come; but when her baby is born she forgets the anguish because of her joy that a child is born into the world.

John 16:21

❧

$\mathcal{C}$hildren's children are a crown to the aged, and parents are the pride of their children.

Proverbs 17:6

❧

$\mathcal{H}$e who fears the LORD has a secure fortress, and for his children it will be a refuge.

Proverbs 14:26

$\mathcal{T}$hese commandments that I give you today are to be upon your hearts. Impress them on your children. Talk about them when you sit at home and when you walk along the road, when you lie down and when you get up.

Deuteronomy 6:6–7

❧

$\mathcal{T}$rain a child in the way he should go, and when he is old he will not turn from it.

Proverbs 22:6

FAMILY

"*Honor* your father and mother"—which
is the first commandment with a promise—"that
it may go well with you and that you may
enjoy long life on the earth."

Ephesians 6:2–3

If anyone does not provide for his relatives, and
especially for his immediate family, he has denied
the faith and is worse than an unbeliever.

1 Timothy 5:8

*C*hildren should not have to save up for their parents, but parents for their children.
2 Corinthians 12:14b

A good man leaves an inheritance for his children's children, but a sinner's wealth is stored up for the righteous.
Proverbs 13:22

*I*f a widow has children or grandchildren, these should learn first of all to put their religion into practice by caring for their own family and so repaying their parents and grandparents, for this is pleasing to God.
1 Timothy 5:4

FRIENDS

*W*ounds from a friend can be trusted.
Proverbs 27:6

*M*y brothers, as believers in our glorious Lord
Jesus Christ, don't show favoritism.
James 2:1

*G*reater love has no one than this, that he lay down
his life for his friends.
John 15:13

$\mathcal{A}$ccept one another, then, just as Christ
accepted you, in order to bring praise to God.
Romans 15:7

$\mathcal{S}$hare with God's people who are in need.
Practice hospitality.
Romans 12:13

$\mathcal{T}$herefore, as we have opportunity, let us do
good to all people, especially to those who belong
to the family of believers.
Galatians 6:10

HEALTH &
BEAUTY

*S*o God created man in his own image, in the image of God he created him; male and female he created them.

Genesis 1:27

*F*or you created my inmost being; you knit me together in my mother's womb. I praise you because I am fearfully and wonderfully made; your works are wonderful, I know that full well.

Psalm 139:13–14

*T*he LORD does not look at the things man looks at. Man looks at the outward appearance, but the LORD looks at the heart.

1 Samuel 16:7

*A*bove all else, guard your heart, for it
is the wellspring of life.
Proverbs 4:23

A cheerful heart is good medicine,
but a crushed spirit dries up the bones.
Proverbs 17:22

*M*y child, be attentive to my words; incline
your ear to my sayings. Do not let them escape
from your sight; keep them within your heart. For
they are life to those who find them, and healing
to all their flesh.
Proverbs 4:20–22 (NRSV)

$\mathcal{Y}$our beauty should not come from outward adornment, such as braided hair and the wearing of gold jewelry and fine clothes. Instead, it should be that of your inner self, the unfading beauty of a gentle and quiet spirit, which is of great worth in God's sight.

1 Peter 3:3–4

$\mathcal{C}$harm is deceptive, and beauty is fleeting; but a woman who fears the LORD is to be praised.

Proverbs 31:30

EMOTIONS

*I*n your anger do not sin: Do not let the
sun go down while you are still angry.
Ephesians 4:26

*B*e kind and compassionate to one
another, forgiving each other, just as
in Christ God forgave you.
Ephesians 4:32

*L*ove your neighbor as yourself.
Leviticus 19:18

$\mathcal{T}$he LORD is my shepherd, I shall not
be in want. Even though I walk through the valley
of the shadow of death, I will fear no evil,
for you are with me; your rod and your staff,
they comfort me.

Psalm 23:1,4

$\mathcal{Y}$our attitude should be the same
as that of Christ Jesus.

Philippians 2:5

*H*ear my cry, O God; listen to my prayer. From the ends of the earth I call to you, I call as my heart grows faint; lead me to the rock that is higher than I. For you have been my refuge, a strong tower against the foe.

Psalm 61:1–3

*C*ast your cares on the LORD and he will sustain you; he will never let the righteous fall.

Psalm 55:22

$\mathscr{D}$o not be anxious about anything, but in everything, by prayer and petition, with thanksgiving, present your requests to God. And the peace of God, which transcends all understanding, will guard your hearts and your minds in Christ Jesus.

Philippians 4:6–7

*P*eace I leave with you; my peace I give you. I do not give to you as the world gives. Do not let your hearts be troubled and do not be afraid.

John 14:27

*A*nd we know that in all things God works for the good of those who love him, who have been called according to his purpose.

Romans 8:28

LIFE'S WORK

$\mathcal{T}$he LORD God took the man and put him in the
Garden of Eden to work it and take care of it.
Genesis 2:15

❧

$\mathcal{Y}$ou will eat the fruit of your labor; blessings
and prosperity will be yours.
Psalm 128:2

$\mathcal{L}$azy hands make a man poor, but diligent
hands bring wealth.
Proverbs 10:4

$\mathcal{A}$ll hard work brings a profit, but mere talk
leads only to poverty.
Proverbs 14:23

*S*ix days you shall labor and do all your work, but the seventh day is a Sabbath to the LORD your God. On it you shall not do any work, neither you, nor your son or daughter, nor your manservant or maidservant, nor your animals, nor the alien within your gates.

Exodus 20:9–10

✢

*M*ake it your ambition to lead a quiet life, to mind your own business and to work with your hands, so that your daily life may win the respect of outsiders and so that you will not be dependent on anybody.

1 Thessalonians 4:11–12

*S*he selects wool and flax and works with
eager hands. She sets about her work vigorously;
her arms are strong for her tasks. Give her
the reward she has earned, and let her
works bring her praise at the city gate.

Proverbs 31:13, 17, 31

*W*hatever you do, work at it with all your heart, as working for the Lord, not for men, since you know that you will receive an inheritance from the Lord as a reward. It is the Lord Christ you are serving.

Colossians 3:23–24

*D*o not work for food that spoils, but for food that endures to eternal life, which the Son of Man will give you. On him God the Father has placed his seal of approval.

John 6:27

We hear that some among you are idle. They are not busy; they are busybodies. Such people we command and urge in the Lord Jesus Christ to settle down and earn the bread they eat. And as for you, brothers, never tire of doing what is right.

2 Thessalonians 3:11–13

❧

*W*hat does the worker gain from his toil?
I know that there is nothing better for men than
to be happy and do good while they live. That
everyone may eat and drink, and find satisfaction
in all his toil—this is the gift of God.

Ecclesiastes 3:9, 12–13

TIME
MANAGEMENT

*T*here is a time for everything, and a season for every activity under heaven: a time to be born and a time to die, a time to plant and a time to uproot, a time to kill and a time to heal, a time to tear down and a time to build, a time to weep and a time to laugh, a time to mourn and a time to dance.

Ecclesiastes 3:1–4

*T*here is a time to scatter stones and a time to gather them, a time to embrace and a time to refrain, a time to search and a time to give up, a time to keep and a time to throw away, a time to tear and a time to mend, a time to be silent and a time to speak, a time to love and a time to hate, a time for war and a time for peace.

Ecclesiastes 3:5–8

*H*e has made everything beautiful in its time. He has also set eternity in the hearts of men; yet they cannot fathom what God has done from beginning to end.

Ecclesiastes 3:11

*D*o not forget this one thing, dear friends: With the Lord a day is like a thousand years, and a thousand years are like a day.

2 Peter 3:8

*M*ay the favor of the Lord our God rest upon us; establish the work of our hands for us—yes, establish the work of our hands.

Psalm 90:17

*D*o not bring a load out of your houses or do any work on the Sabbath, but keep the Sabbath day holy, as I commanded your forefathers.

Jeremiah 17:22

*J*esus answered, "Are there not twelve hours of
daylight? A man who walks by day will
not stumble, for he sees by this world's light.
It is when he walks by night that he stumbles,
for he has no light."

John 11:9–10

*A*s long as it is day, we must do the work
of him who sent me. Night is coming, when
no one can work.

John 9:4

*D*o not boast about tomorrow, for you do not
know what a day may bring forth.

Proverbs 27:1

TOUGH
TIMES

$\mathcal{G}$od is our refuge and strength, an ever-present help in trouble. Therefore we will not fear, though the earth give way and the mountains fall into the heart of the sea, though its waters roar and foam and the mountains quake with their surging.

Psalm 46:1–3

$\mathcal{F}$or in the day of trouble he will keep me safe in his dwelling; he will hide me in the shelter of his tabernacle and set me high upon a rock.

Psalm 27:5

*E*ven though I walk through the valley of the shadow of death, I will fear no evil, for you are with me; your rod and your staff, they comfort me. You prepare a table before me in the presence of my enemies. You anoint my head with oil; my cup overflows.

Psalm 23:4,5

$\mathcal{C}$onsider it pure joy, my brothers, whenever you face trials of many kinds, because you know that the testing of your faith develops perseverance. Perseverance must finish its work so that you may be mature and complete, not lacking anything.

James 1:2–4

*N*o temptation has seized you except what is common to man. And God is faithful; he will not let you be tempted beyond what you can bear. But when you are tempted, he will also provide a way out so that you can stand up under it.

1 Corinthians 10:13

❧

*Y*ou need to persevere so that when you have done the will of God, you will receive what he has promised.

Hebrews 10:36

*N*ot only so, but we also rejoice in our sufferings, because we know that suffering produces perseverance; perseverance, character; and character, hope. And hope does not disappoint us, because God has poured out his love into our hearts by the Holy Spirit, whom he has given us.

Romans 5:3–5

Jesus said, "Blessed are those who are persecuted because of righteousness, for theirs is the kingdom of heaven. Blessed are you when people insult you, persecute you and falsely say all kinds of evil against you because of me. Rejoice and be glad, because great is your reward in heaven, for in the same way they persecuted the prophets who were before you."

Matthew 5:10–12

$\mathcal{A}$s you know, we consider blessed those who have persevered. You have heard of Job's perseverance and have seen what the Lord finally brought about. The Lord is full of compassion and mercy.

James 5:11

❧

$\mathcal{A}$nd the God of all grace, who called you to his eternal glory in Christ, after you have suffered a little while, will himself restore you and make you strong, firm and steadfast.

1 Peter 5:10

MATERIAL
POSSESSIONS

$\mathcal{T}$hen the King will say to those on his right,
"Come, you who are blessed by my Father; take
your inheritance, the kingdom prepared for you
since the creation of the world."

Matthew 25:34

$\mathcal{H}$onor the LORD with your wealth, with
the firstfruits of all your crops; then your barns
will be filled to overflowing, and your vats
will brim over with new wine.

Proverbs 3:9–10

$\mathcal{S}$ome give freely, yet grow all the richer; others withhold what is due, and only suffer want. A generous person will be enriched, and one who gives water will get water.

Proverbs 11:24–25 (NRSV)

$\mathcal{I}$t is well with those who deal generously and lend, who conduct their affairs with justice. For the righteous will never be moved; they will be remembered forever.

Psalm 112:5–6 (NRSV)

$\mathscr{D}$o not store up for yourselves treasures on earth, where moth and rust destroy, and where thieves break in and steal. But store up for yourselves treasures in heaven, where moth and rust do not destroy, and where thieves do not break in and steal. For where your treasure is, there your heart will be also.

Matthew 6:19–21

$\mathcal{P}$eople who want to get rich fall into temptation and a trap and into many foolish and harmful desires that plunge men into ruin and destruction. For the love of money is a root of all kinds of evil. Some people, eager for money, have wandered from the faith and pierced themselves with many griefs.

1 Timothy 6:9–10

*K*eep your lives free from the love of money and be content with what you have, because God has said, "Never will I leave you; never will I forsake you."

Hebrews 13:5

✍

*F*or we brought nothing into the world, and we can take nothing out of it. But if we have food and clothing, we will be content with that.

1 Timothy 6:7–8

*T*his is also why you pay taxes, for the authorities are God's servants, who give their full time to governing. Give everyone what you owe him: If you owe taxes, pay taxes; if revenue, then revenue; if respect, then respect; if honor, then honor. Let no debt remain outstanding, except the continuing debt to love one another, for he who loves his fellowman has fulfilled the law.

Romans 13:6–8

$\mathcal{D}$o not love the world or the things of the world. The love of the Father is not in those who love the world; for all that is in the world—the desire of the flesh, the desires of the eyes, the pride in riches—comes not from the Father but from the world. And the world and its desire are passing away, but those who do the will of God live forever.

1 John 2:15–17 (NRSV)